GW00467825

BOOK ANALYSIS

By Jule Lenzen

The Portrait of a Lady

BY HENRY JAMES

Bright
Summaries.com

HENRY JAMES

- **Born in New York City in 1843.**
- **Died in Chelsea, England in 1916.**
- **Notable works:**
  - *The American* (1877), novel
  - *The Golden Bowl* (1904), novel
  - *Notes of a Son and Brother* (1914), memoir

Henry James Junior, as he was known during his lifetime, was the son of famous theologian Henry James Senior. He had four siblings, and particularly his elder brother William and his younger sister Alice, who was an invalid, were important figures in his life. Already during his childhood, he and his family travelled extensively in Europe, a habit which he continued in his later life, travelling to Italy, Switzerland and France, among other countries. In 1875 James decided to move to Europe, and in 1876 he permanently settled in England.

James took his art very seriously, and in 1884 he proclaimed his intention to remain a bachelor in order to devote his time to his writing. Apart from his numerous novels, he wrote 112 short stories, various travel memoirs and critical essays on literature. James endeavoured to live from his writing and during his lifetime frequently found himself in economically precarious situations. For this reason, he also started to write plays in 1890, a largely unsuccessful endeavour.

In his later years, he was increasingly ill. From 1897 onwards, he employed a typist due to rheumatism in his wrist. In 1915, a year before his death, James became a British citizen, partly in order to protest against America's neutrality in the First World War. James was awarded the Order of Merit in 1916, shortly before his death. Both James' literary works and his literary criticism have had an enormous impact on subsequent generations of writers. The complexity of James' works has earned him the title of "writer's writer" (Horne 2004: 19).

THE PORTRAIT OF A LADY

AMERICAN INNOCENCE CLASHES WITH THE TRADITIONS OF OLD EUROPE

- **Genre:** novel
- **Reference edition:** James, H. (2014) *The Portrait of a Lady*. London: Penguin Books.
- **1st edition:** 1881
- **Themes:** innocence, Americans in Europe, betrayal, displacement, Modernism, Victorian literature

In order to write *The Portrait of a Lady*, James saved money for several years and began writing the novel in 1880: "[...] James was consciously pulling together many of his previous experiences in life and achievements in art, and deliberately setting out to compose a masterpiece [...]" (Horne, 2014: xv). The novel was published in serial form both in the *Atlantic* in the US and in *Macmillan's Magazine* in England (*ibid.*: 6). The main character of *The Portrait of a Lady* (and of many of James' other novels) was inspired by James' cousin Minnie Temple, who died at an early age (*ibid.*: xvi).

In 1908, James undertook the reworking of most of his literary works in their New York editions, and *The Portrait of a Lady* also underwent several changes. The reference edition used in this guide is based on the original text of 1881.

SUMMARY

The novel follows the development of the young American Isabel Archer, who accompanies her aunt Lydia Touchett from Albany to England, and later inherits a large sum of money from her uncle Mr. Touchett. Her money attracts the fortune hunter Gilbert Osmond, who convinces her to marry him. The novel shows her transition from a young, free and independent girl into a dependent and unhappy woman. Prominent within the novel is the frequent contrasting of new, innocent America and old, conventional Europe.

ISABEL IN ENGLAND

The novel opens with a very British convention in a very British setting: afternoon tea at Gardencourt, the home of Mr. Touchett and his son, Ralph Touchett. Lord Warburton, the proprietor of a nearby mansion and a member of the British aristocracy, is visiting them. This set-up already contrasts both worlds in the very first chapter. Isabel Archer arrives with her aunt from America. During her stay at Gardencourt, she establishes close friendships with her uncle and with her sickly cousin Ralph. Ralph makes her the object of his life: he determines to observe her progress in life, and therefore also asks his dying father to leave her a large inheritance in his will.

Isabel charms the men she comes across. She rejects a marriage proposal by the rich Lord Warburton, and also by the American Caspar Goodwood, who has followed her from America. She promises the latter that she will reconsider his proposal in two years' time. While old Mr. Touchett is dying, Madame Merle, an old friend of Mrs. Touchett from Florence, comes to stay. She and Isabel establish a close friendship. Upon learning of Isabel's large inheritance a few weeks later, it becomes immediately apparent that this greatly increases Isabel's appeal to Merle.

ISABEL IN ITALY

After having inherited the large fortune from her uncle, Isabel accompanies her aunt to her house in Florence. Here, Madame Merle executes her ingenious plan of marrying Isabel and Gilbert Osmond, an old friend of Merle. Isabel is introduced to Osmond and his daughter Pansy, as well as his sister, the Countess Gemini. The Countess tries to warn Isabel about Osmond, but Madame Merle takes care to discredit her in front of Isabel. Ralph does not believe that Isabel could marry Osmond, while Mrs. Touchett enlists Madame Merle's help in trying to stop the engagement, unaware that Merle is playing a double game. During a visit to Rome with her friends Henrietta Stackpole and Ralph, Isabel meets Lord Warburton again, and again dismisses him. It is also during this visit that Osmond declares his love for her. After this, Isabel travels around the world for a year, occasionally accompanied by her sister from America and by Madame Merle. At the close of the year, she decides to marry Osmond. The reader learns of this during a subsequent conversation between Isabel and Goodwood, who is immensely disappointed and travels from America to Italy in order to see Isabel. Her nearest relations and friends are also immensely disappointed in Isabel's choice, but Isabel repeatedly states that she is not marrying to please other people (p. 346). Ralph tries to warn Isabel about Osmond, which results in a cooling of their friendship, since Isabel refuses to hear anything against Osmond.

After an interval of four years, the reader is gradually introduced to Isabel's (now Mrs. Osmond) new life in Rome. She lives at the Palazzo Roccanera with Osmond and Pansy and holds regular evening gatherings. Gradually, it is revealed how unhappy Isabel is in her marriage. Osmond tried to manipulate and form her, just as he did with his daughter, but Isabel has always resisted this and therefore Osmond hates her. Isabel cannot confide in any of her old friends (Ralph, Lord Warburton or Caspar Goodwood), who all make their appearance in Rome, having formerly dismissed all their warnings. The only person she can confide in is Henrietta. Henrietta wants to make Isabel promise to leave Osmond "before the worst comes" (p. 528). At the same time, Pansy has multiple suitors: Edward Rosier (an old friend of Isabel's from Paris), whose feelings Pansy returns, is deemed by Osmond not good (rich) enough for his daughter. Lord Warburton also shows his interest, which greatly pleases both Osmond and Mme Merle. Warburton eventually returns to England, and Osmond and Mme Merle blame Isabel for this. Pansy is sent to a convent to make her submissive to her father. Isabel receives a message from Gardencourt that Ralph is dying and determines to travel to England immediately. This results in an open confrontation between her and Osmond. Isabel finally learns from the Countess Gemini why Osmond and Merle are so close: Pansy is their daughter. This decides Isabel, and she takes the next train to England, after having visited Pansy at the convent and promised her to return. In a final conflict with Mme Merle, the latter announces that she will go to America.

GARDENCOURT

Upon her return to England, Isabel learns of multiple engagements: Henrietta and Mr Bantling are to marry, and Lord Warburton has finally got engaged to an English lady. Isabel and Ralph manage to talk openly to one another while Ralph is dying. He wants Isabel to be happy. Isabel sees the ghost at Gardencourt, which was mentioned in the opening chapters of the novel as only visible to those who have suffered, marking her transition from the young, happy girl she once was. Caspar Goodwood comes to visit Isabel at

Gardencourt, professes his love for her and asks her not to return to Rome, but to stay with him. They kiss. A few days later, Goodwood learns from Henrietta that Isabel has boarded a train for Rome.

CHARACTER STUDY

At the beginning of the novel, Isabel Archer, is an American innocent. She is very independent and enjoys her liberty (p. 70). She knows her own mind and is witty, self-confident and sharp. As the niece of Mrs. Touchett, she is introduced to Europe. Her independence is partly the result of both of her parents being dead. She has two sisters in America. Isabel is accomplished: she loves to read and has a natural taste for art (p. 47), which again underlines her innocence – her taste has not been influenced by tradition. Isabel is very intelligent and has a great hunger for knowledge, which she tries to satisfy by travelling. She states herself: "[...] I don't want to begin life by marrying. There are other things a woman can do" (p. 157). She has a passion for justice (p. 567), and throughout the novel there is great emphasis on Isabel's imagination (p. 51). She also has a great love for children (p. 148), which foreshadows her great devotion to Osmond's daughter Pansy. At a later stage, "her tenderness for things pure and weak" (p. 427) is highlighted. Isabel's innocence and naiveté ultimately make her the victim of Madame Merle and Gilbert Osmond.

Isabel's marriage to Osmond greatly changes this free and innocent young woman. This is the first glimpse the reader receives of the changed Isabel through the eyes of Edward Rosier, and already hints at Osmond's transformative effect on her character:

> "The years had touched her only to enrich her; the flower of her youth had not faded, it only hung more quietly on its stem. She had lost something of that quick eagerness to which her husband had privately taken exception – she had more the air of being able to wait. Now at all events, framed in the gilded doorway, she struck our young man as the picture of a gracious lady." (p. 387)

We later see the effect her marriage to Osmond has had on her: "Her faculties, her energy, her passion, were all dispersed again; she felt as if a cold, dark mist had suddenly encompassed her" (p. 568). She has grown sarcastic and depressed.

Isabel's former optimism (p. 52) turns to pessimism in the course of her marriage.

GILBERT OSMOND

Osmond, as he is mostly referred to in the novel, is a widowed American who has spent most of his life in Europe, and mostly in Italy. He is about 40 years old and has a house in Florence where he lives with his daughter Pansy. The reader automatically supposes her to be his daughter from his first marriage, but later learns that he had an affair with the married Mme Merle, who is Pansy's mother. Osmond is poor and has no occupation but delights in collecting fine objects – among which he also counts his daughter and later his wife.

He refers to himself as thoroughly European when he states: "No, I am not conventional; I am convention itself" (p. 327). At first Isabel is charmed by Osmond: she supposes him to be the ultimate gentleman, intelligent and accomplished. And while he is all that, her view of him changes in her marriage: she highlights his egotism, his snobbery and his contempt for everyone and everything (p. 452). Most importantly, however, Osmond is controlling, and he hates Isabel because: "The real offence, as she ultimately perceived, was her having a mind of her own at all" (p. 454).

In their marriage, Osmond tries to psychologically manipulate Isabel: he pretends to like Goodwood (p. 520) or sends his daughter to a convent (p. 561) simply to disconcert and provoke Isabel. He forbids Isabel to go and see her dying cousin, since he dislikes Ralph (knowing that Ralph has seen through him and will endeavour to protect Isabel).

MADAME MERLE

Like Osmond, Madame Merle is an alienated American. She has lived abroad for a long time, so that when Isabel first meets her, she does not recognise her as a fellow countrywoman (p. 184). She is around 40 years old and is a very accomplished and intelligent woman. Isabel immediately takes her as a role model and strikes up a close friendship with her.

Madame Merle is also clever in conversation: when she makes a mistake, she does not retract, but changes her statement so that it seems natural (p. 218). She is very cunning. Moreover, she is shown to be cold and calculating: she sets up Isabel to marry Osmond in order to secure a fortune for her illegitimate daughter Pansy. After having been found out by Isabel, Mme Merle announces her intention to go to America (p. 589).

ANALYSIS

As highlighted in the summary section of this guide, the novel repeatedly contrasts American innocence with old Europe. Several of the characters serve to signify one of the sides. There is also the category of the alienated or Europeanized American, to which both Gilbert Osmond and Serena Merle belong.

America is characterised by innocence and newness ('the New World'), while Europe is represented by traditions and conventions. In the beginning, Isabel Archer clearly conforms to the image of the innocent American, as she has a natural taste and in her dealings with other people repeatedly shows her innocence:

> "Mrs. Touchett fixed her bright little eyes upon him for a moment, and then transferred them to her niece. 'You can't stay alone with the gentlemen. You are not – you are not at Albany, my dear.' Isabel rose, blushing." (p. 69)

Caspar Goodwood is another example of the archetypal American, and is even classified as such by other characters (p. 355). On the other hand, the aristocratic Lord Warburton is the archetypal European: he is the personification of European tradition.

The case of the Europeanized American is more complex: on the surface, these characters seem to represent the Old World, with Osmond stating, for example, that he is the personification of convention (p. 327). However, Merle and Osmond's American roots lend a falsity to the characters. Other supposedly Europeanized characters such as the Touchetts are still shown to be American at heart, while Merle and Osmond have both completely assimilated: "The Touchetts are not English at all, you know; they live on a kind of foreign system; they have some awfully queer ideas" (p. 149). And even Mrs. Touchett, who can neither be classified as innocent nor is as reluctant to assimilate to European customs as the male members of her family, has a defect of her own: she lacks emotion (Horne, 2014: xv).

By making those American characters that completely assimilate to the old European ways in some way faulty, Henry James manages to make a strong statement on displacement and its psychological consequences.

Horne takes the contrast even further in seeing it as a statement on the novel's transition between Victorian and Modernist literary traditions: "[...] negotiating between what could be broadly seen as the European past of social fixity and hierarchy and the American future of industrial and territorial expansion" (*ibid.*: xiv).

VICTORIAN AND MODERNIST ELEMENTS

Victorian literature

- **Period:** 1837-1901
- **Features of the Victorian novel:** 3-volume novel; serialisation in magazines; self-consciousness and self-analysis; contradictions (Enlightenment vs. religion)
- **Important writers:** Charles Dickens, Sir Arthur Conan Doyle, the Brontë sisters

Modernist literature

- **Period:** early-mid-20th century
- **Features of the (early) Modernist novel:** challenging previous literary conventions; influence of psychoanalysis; experimentation with form; trying to reflect movement and scale associated with modern times; influence of WW1
- **Important writers:** Virginia Woolf, T. S. Eliot, James Joyce

The Portrait of a Lady has been described as combining features of Victorian and Modernist literature: "it [the novel] represents a dialogue between Victorian certainties and modernist doubts" (Horne, 2014: xiii). Victorian elements in the novel can be seen in its formal structure: it was originally published in three volumes, which was a popular format in early Victorian times (*ibid.*). Moreover, the narrator shows great self-awareness – the narrative voice often directly addresses the reader and comments on the narration process:

> "It is not, however, during this interval that we are closely concerned with her; our attention is

engaged again on a certain day in the late spring-time [...] a year from the date of the incidents I have just narrated." (p. 335)

Moreover, *The Portrait of a Lady* has several Gothic elements. This form of the novel was practised by the Victorian Brontë sisters (Shrimpton, 2017: n.p.), among others. James' novel mentions a ghost (p. 48), and the descriptions of certain places such as the Palazzo Roccanera reflect those in Gothic novels (p. 384).

However, James' extreme preoccupation with the aesthetics of his novel, which also resulted in his decision to rework it for the New York edition, is a feature of Modernist literature. Moreover, the influence of psychoanalysis on his novel can clearly be seen: there is an immense preoccupation with the inner lives of his characters and, as has been highlighted in the characterisation of Osmond, with the psychological manipulation of others.

Modernist literature is usually seen as beginning after the First World War, and as such Henry James is not usually mentioned in the canon of Modernist writers, although his work exhibits certain Modernist elements.

PORTRAYAL OF A LADY

The novel contains multiple references to Isabel in the form of a portrait, reflecting its title. Some of the other female characters are also alluded to in this way, most notably Pansy Osmond. In many ways, her characterisation reflects that of Isabel in the beginning: one of the nuns from the convent describes her by saying "She is perfect. She has no faults" (p. 242). This is mirrored by a similar observation made by Osmond on Isabel:

> "He thought Miss Archer sometimes too eager, too pronounced. It was a pity she had that fault; because if she had not had it she really would have none; she would have been as bright and soft as an April cloud." (p. 318)

Just some of the examples of how Isabel is treated by others as a portrait include the following: when Goodwood travels to Italy to see her, she asks him: "Do you mean that you came simply to look at me?" (p. 348); and at the very beginning of the novel, Ralph looks at Isabel rather than at the portraits in the gallery of his house (p. 47).

What is more, many of the people surrounding Isabel seem to watch her life as if it were a play, a theme alluded to multiple times in the novel: both Ralph and Merle state, independently of one another, that they want to see what becomes of Isabel.

Building on the idea of a portrait, at the end of the novel Isabel is repeatedly referred to as an angel (p. 505), and even as Madonna (p. 494). This introduces a religious notion that is also apparent in Pansy, who is sent twice to the convent.

However, the reader gains insight into Isabel's thoughts and feelings, which shows her to be more than a portrait, even though that is how the other characters in the novel choose to look at her.

While the description of Pansy in many ways reflects that of Isabel, her characterisation takes the idea of a portrait even further: Pansy is purely decorative, devoid of her own personality and easy to form. Madame Catherine says that "*Elle éclaire la maison*" (p. 583) ("She brightens the house"), thereby highlighting Pansy's decorative function. Moreover, we are given no insight into

Pansy's thought processes. The following quote shows how Osmond endeavours to make his daughter into a perfect piece of art:

> "[...] and to show that if he regarded his daughter as a precious work of art, it was natural he should be more and more careful about the finishing touches. If he wished to be effective he had succeeded; the incident struck a chill into Isabel's heart." (p. 561)

While Isabel resists the aestheticizing of herself into a portrait, Pansy in the end succumbs to her father's wishes and becomes submissive: "Isabel read the meaning of it; she saw that the poor girl had been vanquished" (p. 586).

FURTHER REFLECTION

SOME QUESTIONS TO THINK ABOUT...

- Why do you think Isabel marries Osmond? Is it out of a maternal sense of duty towards his daughter, or as she herself states, "she had really married on a factitious theory, in order to do something finely appreciable with her money" (p. 450)?
- Why do you think Isabel returns to Rome at the end of the novel, rather than beginning a new life with Caspar Goodwood? Has she become Europeanized and therefore rejects the idea of divorce? Or is this Osmond's Catholic influence?
- Apart from Isabel and Pansy, would you say that the other female characters in the novel are also represented as portraits? Explain your answer.
- Would you say the depiction of female characters greatly differs from that of male characters? See for example the repeated emphasis

of female characters being perfect, such as Ralph's statement on Madame Merle: "She is perfect; she is the only woman I know who has but that one little fault" (p. 263).

- Given the analysis above, do you think the title of the novel refers to Isabel or to Pansy? Explain your answer.
- Many of James' characters have 'telling names', such as 'Henrietta Stackpole', 'Caspar Goodwood' or 'Pansy'. What do these names say about the characters?
- Is Pansy an American or a European, or neither? Explain your answer.
- What is the significance of the various houses, such as the Palazzo Roccanera or Gardencourt? Do they represent their occupiers?

We want to hear from you!
Leave a comment on your online library
and share your favourite books on social media!

FURTHER READING

REFERENCE EDITION

- James, H. (2014) *The Portrait of a Lady*. London: Penguin Books.

REFERENCE STUDIES

- Horne, P. (2004) James, Henry. *Oxford DNB*. [Online]. [Accessed 15 November 2018]. Available from: <https://doi.org/10.1093/ref:odnb/34150>
- Horne, P. (2014) Introduction. In James, H. *The Portrait of a Lady*. London: Penguin Books.
- Horne, P. (2014) Chronology. In James, H. *The Portrait of a Lady*. London: Penguin Books.
- Shrimpton, N. et al. (2017) English Literature. *Encyclopaedia Brittannica*. [Online]. [Accessed 22 November 2018]. Available from: <https://www.britannica.com/art/English-literature>

ADDITIONAL SOURCES

- Edel, L. (1985) *Henry James: A Life*. New York: Harper.

- Freedman, J. ed. (1998) *The Cambridge Companion to Henry James*. Cambridge: Cambridge University Press.

- Horne, P. (1990) *Henry James and Revision: The New York Edition*. Oxford: Oxford University Press.

- James, H. (1984) *Literary Criticism*. New York: Cambridge University Press.

- James, H. (1922) *The Novels and Tales of Henry James*. New York: Scribner.

- Porte, J. ed. (1990) *New Essays on The Portrait of a Lady*. Cambridge: Cambridge University Press.

- Stafford, W. T. ed. (1967) *Perspectives on James's The Portrait of a Lady: A Collection of Critical Essays*. New York: New York University Press.

ADAPTATIONS

- *The Portrait of a Lady*. (1954) [Play]. William Archibald. New York City: ANTA Playhouse.

- *The Portrait of a Lady*. (1968) [TV miniseries]. James Cellan Jones. Dir. United Kingdom: BBC.

- *The Portrait of a Lady*. (1996) [Film]. Jane Campion. Dir. United Kingdom and USA: Umbrella Entertainment.

MORE FROM BRIGHTSUMMARIES.COM

- Reading guide – *The Turn of the Screw* by Henry James.

- Reading guide – *What Maisie Knew* by Henry James.

Bright ≡Summaries.com

More guides to rediscover your love of literature

- Animal Farm — BY GEORGE ORWELL
- The Stranger — BY ALBERT CAMUS
- Harry Potter and the Sorcerer's Stone — BY J.K. ROWLING
- The Silence of the Sea — BY VERCORS
- Antigone — BY JEAN ANOUILH
- The Flowers of Evil — BY BAUDELAIRE

www.brightsummaries.com

Ebook EAN: 9782808015653

Paperback EAN: 9782808015660

Legal Deposit: D/2018/12603/541

Cover: © Primento

Digital conception by Primento, the digital partner of
publishers.

Lightning Source UK Ltd.
Milton Keynes UK
UKHW020816300822
408024UK00012B/2610